Type 1 Diab.....s
Cookbook for Kids

(100 delicious recipes kids love to eat)

Sonia Russell

TABLE OF CONTENTS

CHAPTER 1   9

   **Understanding Type 1 Diabetes in Children
and the Importance of Nutrition**   9

CHAPTER 2   17

   **Meal Planning strategies for Type 1 Diabetes
Kids**   17

CHAPTER 3   25

   **Breakfast Recipes for Kids with Type 1
Diabetes**   25

   Overnight Oats with Berries   25

   Poached Eggs and Spinach on Toast   27

   Greek Yogurt Parfait   30

   Banana Oat Pancakes   32

   Veggie Frittata   35

   Peanut Butter and Banana Toast   38

   Baked Oatmeal Cups   40

   Whole Wheat Waffles   43

   Fruit and Yogurt Smoothie   46

   Avocado Toast   48

   Egg and Cheese Burrito   50

   Ham and Cheese Breakfast Sandwich   52

   Egg Muffins   53

   Mug Omelet   55

   Quinoa Porridge   57

CHAPTER 4   **61**

**Snack Ideas to keep Kids with Type 1
Diabetes fueled throughout the day**   61

Hard-boiled Eggs with a sprinkle of Sea Salt   61

Fruit Smoothie with Greek Yogurt and Chia Seeds 62

Whole Wheat Toast with Almond Butter and Banana
Slices   63

Celery Sticks with Cream Cheese and Raisins   64

Hummus and Vegetables   65

Peanut Butter and Jelly on Whole Wheat Bread   66

Baked Kale Chips   67

Popcorn with Olive Oil and a Sprinkle of Parmesan
Cheese   69

Veggie Chips and Hummus   70

Whole Wheat Pretzels with Nut Butter   71

Baked Sweet Potato Chips with a Sprinkle of
Cinnamon   72

Apple Slices with Almond Butter   73

Turkey and Cheese Roll-Ups   74

Trail Mix with Dark Chocolate Chips   75

Cheese and Crackers   76

CHAPTER 5   **79**

Kid-Approved Lunch recipes for T1D   79

Chicken Quesadillas   79

Mediterranean Wrap   81

Peanut Butter and Banana Sandwich   82

Turkey and Cheddar Sandwich   83

Hummus Wrap   84

Cheese and Spinach Quesadilla 85

Egg and Cheese Sandwich 87

Veggie Wrap 89

Cheese Pizza 90

Tuna Sandwich 92

Cheesy Pasta 93

Egg Salad Sandwich 95

Macaroni and Cheese 96

Grilled Cheese Sandwich 97

Whole Wheat Pita Pizza 98

CHAPTER 6 **101**

Easy Dinner Recipes for T1D kids 101

Macaroni and Cheese 101

Cheesy Baked Tortellini 102

Baked Fish Fingers 104

Cheesy Broccoli Rice 105

Baked Zucchini Fries 107

Baked Chicken Nuggets 108

Mini Veggie Pizzas 110

Turkey Sloppy Joes 111

Baked Chicken Tenders 113

Grilled Cheese Sandwiches 114

Roasted Vegetables 116

Baked Potato Wedges 117

Baked Sweet Potato Fries 118

Creamy Chicken Alfredo 120

CHAPTER 7 **123**

Satisfying Type 1 Diabetes-friendly Desserts

for kids 123

Banana Split 123

Baked Apple 125

Chocolate Peanut Butter Rice Krispie Treats 126

Apple Pie Crisp 128

Chocolate Peanut Butter Banana Popsicles 129

Oatmeal Raisin Cookies 131

Coconut Macaroons 133

Fruit Pizza 135

Chocolate Banana Boats 136

Fruit and Yogurt Parfait 138

Chocolate-Dipped Strawberries 139

Chocolate Peanut Butter Fudge 141

Cinnamon Apple Chips 142

Peanut Butter and Jelly Bars 144

CHAPTER 8 **147**

Dealing with Eating outside the home with your T1D kids 147

CHAPTER 9 **151**

Coping mechanisms for parents of kids with T1D 151

CHAPTER 10 **157**

Conclusion and Additional Resources for Families of Kids with Type 1 Diabetes 157

Additional Resources 158

Diabetes Education **161**

Diabetes Foot Care Education **162**

BONUS **163**

14 Days Meal Planner   163
Thank You Note   167

CHAPTER 1

Understanding Type 1 Diabetes in Children and the Importance of Nutrition

Type 1 diabetes is a chronic condition that affects millions of children around the world. It is an autoimmune disorder in which the body's immune system mistakenly attacks and destroys the insulin-producing cells of the pancreas.

Without insulin, the body cannot access the sugar it needs for energy, causing high levels of sugar in the blood and leading to serious, life-threatening health issues. Fortunately, with the right care and dietary management, children with type 1 diabetes can lead healthy, active lives.

Type 1 diabetes is an autoimmune disorder that can affect children of all ages. It is caused when the body's immune system mistakenly attacks and destroys the insulin-producing cells of the pancreas, leading to an inability to produce insulin.

Without insulin, the body cannot access the sugar it needs for energy, and blood sugar levels become dangerously high. This can lead to a number of health issues, including kidney failure, nerve damage, heart disease, and stroke.

Type 1 diabetes is usually diagnosed in children between the ages of 4 and 14, although it can occur at any age. Symptoms of type 1 diabetes can include excessive thirst and urination, fatigue, weight loss, and blurry vision. If any of these symptoms are present, it is important to see a doctor for an accurate diagnosis.

Nutrition is key to managing type 1 diabetes in children. Children with type 1 diabetes must closely monitor their intake of carbohydrates, proteins, and fats to keep their blood sugar levels in a safe range.

They should also limit their intake of processed and sugary foods, as these can cause spikes in blood sugar. Eating a balanced diet that is high in fruits and vegetables, lean proteins, whole grains, and healthy fats is recommended.

Children with type 1 diabetes should also monitor their intake of sodium, as high levels of this mineral can increase blood pressure and put additional strain on the heart. It is also important to ensure adequate hydration.

Drinking enough water, as well as eating foods with high water content, will help to keep the body hydrated and also help to regulate blood sugar levels.

Type 1 diabetes is a serious, life-threatening condition that affects millions of children around the world. With the right care and dietary management, however, children with type 1 diabetes can lead healthy, active lives.

Nutrition is key to managing type 1 diabetes in children, and it is important to ensure they are eating a balanced diet that is high in fruits and vegetables, lean proteins, whole grains, and healthy fats.

Drinking enough water and limiting processed and sugary foods are also important for managing type 1 diabetes. With the right care, children with type 1 diabetes can lead happy and healthy lives.

CHAPTER 2

Meal Planning strategies for Type 1 Diabetes Kids

Meal planning strategies for Type 1 diabetes kids can be a daunting task for any parent.

This is especially true if the parent is unfamiliar with the complexity of managing diabetes and the dietary needs of a child with diabetes. Planning meals for a child with Type 1 diabetes requires a great deal of attention and dedication to ensure that their dietary needs are being met.

This cookbook will provide parents with an overview of meal planning strategies for Type 1 diabetes kids, with a focus on the importance of creating healthy and balanced meals.

First and foremost, it is important for parents to understand the basics of Type 1 diabetes and the dietary needs of their child.

Type 1 diabetes is an autoimmune disorder, which means that the body's own immune system attacks and destroys the cells in the pancreas that produce insulin. Insulin is a hormone that is essential for the body to be able to use the glucose in food for energy. Without insulin, the body can't use glucose and the child will experience high blood sugar levels.

To manage this, children with Type 1 diabetes need to take insulin injections or use an insulin pump. In addition to this, they also need to follow a healthy and balanced diet to help keep their blood sugar levels in check.

When it comes to meal planning for a child with Type 1 diabetes, it is important to understand that the goal is to create meals that are balanced in terms of carbohydrates, proteins, and fats.

Carbohydrates are the main source of energy for the body, and the type and amount of carbohydrates that a child eats can have a significant impact on their blood sugar levels.

It is important to include a variety of carbohydrates in the diet, such as fruits, vegetables, grains, beans, and dairy products. It is also important to limit processed and sugary foods, as these can raise blood sugar levels quickly.

In addition to focusing on carbohydrates, it is also important to include an adequate amount of protein in the diet. Protein helps to slow the absorption of glucose into the bloodstream, which can help to prevent blood sugar spikes. Good sources of protein include lean meats, fish, eggs, nuts, and beans.

Fats are also important for providing energy and helping to slow the absorption of glucose, and should be included in the diet in moderate amounts. Good sources of healthy fats include avocados, nuts, and seeds, as well as certain oils such as olive oil and coconut oil.

When planning meals for a child with Type 1 diabetes, it is important to keep in mind that portion sizes are important. Eating too much or too little can have an impact on blood sugar levels, so it is important to make sure that portion sizes are appropriate for the child's age and activity level.

It is also important to include snacks throughout the day to help keep blood sugar levels stable, such as a piece of fruit or a handful of nuts.

Finally, it is important to be aware of the signs and symptoms of low blood sugar, which can include dizziness, confusion, and fatigue. It is important to be prepared with a source of fast-acting sugar, such as glucose tablets or fruit juice, in case of a low blood sugar episode.

In conclusion, meal planning strategies for Type 1 diabetes kids can be a difficult and time-consuming task for parents. However, with the proper understanding of diabetes and the dietary needs of the child, parents can create healthy and balanced meals that will help to keep their child's blood sugar levels in check.

By paying attention to portion sizes, including snacks throughout the day, and being prepared for low blood sugar episodes, parents can help ensure that their child has the nutrition they need to stay healthy and active.

CHAPTER 3

Breakfast Recipes for Kids with Type 1 Diabetes

Overnight Oats with Berries

Ingredients:

-2/3 cup of oats

-1/2 cup of low-fat milk

-1/4 cup of fresh or frozen berries

-1 tablespoon of honey

-1 teaspoon of chia seeds

Preparation Method:

-In a bowl, mix together the oats, milk, honey, and chia seeds.

-Cover the bowl with a lid or plastic wrap and place in the refrigerator overnight.

-In the morning, top with the berries.

Nutritional Information (per serving):

-Calories: 335

-Carbohydrates: 56g

-Protein: 10g

-Fat: 5g

Preparation Time: 5 minutes (plus overnight)

Serving Size: 1 bowl

Poached Eggs and Spinach on Toast

Ingredients:

-2 eggs

-1 teaspoon of white vinegar

-1/2 cup of baby spinach

-2 slices of whole wheat toast

-1 tablespoon of olive oil

Preparation Method

-Fill a shallow pan with an inch of water and bring to a boil.

-Add the vinegar and reduce the heat to a simmer.

-Crack the eggs into the water and cook for 3-4 minutes.

-Meanwhile, heat the olive oil in a skillet over medium heat.

-Add the spinach and sauté for a few minutes until wilted.

-Toast the bread slices and top with the spinach and poached eggs.

Nutritional Information (per serving):

-Calories: 390

-Carbohydrates: 35g

-Protein: 19g

-Fat: 20g

Preparation Time: 10 minutes

Serving Size: 4 servings

Greek Yogurt Parfait

Ingredients:

-1/2 cup of Greek yogurt

-1/2 cup of granola

-1/4 cup of fresh berries

-1 teaspoon of honey

Preparation Method:

-Layer the yogurt, granola, and berries in a bowl.

-Top with a drizzle of honey.

Nutritional Information (per serving):

-Calories: 280

-Carbohydrates: 41g

-Protein: 14g

-Fat: 7g

Preparation Time: 5 minutes

Serving Size: 1 bowl

Banana Oat Pancakes

Ingredients:

-1 ripe banana

-1/2 cup of oats

-1/2 cup of low-fat milk

-1 egg

-1 teaspoon of baking powder

-1 teaspoon of cinnamon

-1 tablespoon of olive oil

Preparation Method:

-In a blender, puree the banana, oats, milk, egg, baking powder, and cinnamon until smooth.

-Heat the olive oil in a skillet over medium heat.

-Pour the batter into the skillet in small circles and cook for 2-3 minutes on each side until golden brown.

Nutritional Information (per serving):

-Calories: 325

-Carbohydrates: 56g

-Protein: 13g

-Fat: 8g

Preparation Time: 10 minutes

Serving Size: 2 pancakes

Veggie Frittata

Ingredients:

-1/4 cup of diced onion

-1/4 cup of diced bell pepper

-1/4 cup of diced mushrooms

-2 tablespoons of grated cheese

-3 eggs

-1/4 cup of low-fat milk

-1 tablespoon of olive oil

Preparation Method:

-Heat the olive oil in a skillet over medium heat.

-Add the onion, bell pepper, and mushrooms and sauté for a few minutes until softened.

-In a bowl, whisk together the eggs and milk.

-Add the egg mixture to the skillet and cook for 2-3 minutes until the edges begin to set.

-Sprinkle the cheese over the top and cook for another 2-3 minutes until set in the center.

Nutritional Information (per serving):

-Calories: 146

-Carbohydrates: 4g

-Protein: 11g

-Fat: 10g

Preparation Time: 15 minutes

Serving Size: 3 Frittatas

Peanut Butter and Banana Toast

Ingredients:

-2 slices of whole wheat toast

-2 tablespoons of peanut butter

-1 banana, sliced

-1 teaspoon of honey

Preparation Method:

-Toast the bread slices.

-Spread the peanut butter on the toast and top with the banana slices.

-Drizzle with honey.

Nutritional Information (per serving):

-Calories: 305

-Carbohydrates: 37g

-Protein: 11g

-Fat: 14g

Preparation Time: 5 minutes

Serving Size: 2 slices of toast

Baked Oatmeal Cups

Ingredients:

-1/2 cup of oats

-1/4 cup of low-fat milk

-1/4 cup of yogurt

-1 egg

-1/4 cup of dried cranberries

-1/4 teaspoon of cinnamon

Preparation Method:

-Preheat the oven to 350°F.

-In a bowl, mix together the oats, milk, yogurt, egg, cranberries, and cinnamon.

-Grease a muffin tin and pour the mixture into the cups, filling about 3/4 of the way.

-Bake for 15-20 minutes until golden brown.

Nutritional Information (per serving):

-Calories: 126

-Carbohydrates: 21g

-Protein: 6g

-Fat: 3g

Preparation Time: 10 minutes

Serving Size: 4 muffin cups

Whole Wheat Waffles

Ingredients:

-1/2 cup of whole wheat flour

-1/2 teaspoon of baking powder

-1/4 teaspoon of baking soda

-2 tablespoons of honey

-1 egg

-1/2 cup of low-fat milk

-1 tablespoon of olive oil

Preparation Method:

-In a bowl, mix together the flour, baking powder, baking soda, and honey.

-In a separate bowl, whisk together the egg, milk, and oil.

-Add the wet ingredients to the dry ingredients and mix until just combined.

-Heat a waffle iron and pour the batter into the iron.

-Cook for 3-4 minutes until golden brown.

Nutritional Information (per serving):

-Calories: 286

-Carbohydrates: 43g

-Protein: 9g

-Fat: 9g

Preparation Time: 10 minutes

Serving Size: Two waffles

Fruit and Yogurt Smoothie

Ingredients:

-1/2 cup of Greek yogurt

-1/2 cup of frozen fruit

-1/2 cup of low-fat milk

-1 teaspoon of honey

Preparation Method:

-Place all ingredients in a blender and blend until smooth.

Nutritional Information (per serving):

-Calories: 150

-Carbohydrates: 22g

-Protein: 9g

-Fat: 3g

Preparation Time: 5 minutes

Serving Size: 1 smoothie

Avocado Toast

Ingredients:

-1/4 of an avocado

-1 teaspoon of lime juice

-2 slices of whole wheat toast

-1/2 cup of baby spinach

Preparation Method:

-Mash the avocado in a bowl and add the lime juice.

-Spread the mixture on the toast and top with the spinach.

Nutritional Information (per serving):

-Calories: 155

-Carbohydrates: 22g

-Protein: 5g

-Fat: 8g

Preparation Time: 5 minutes

Serving Size: 1 serving (2 slices of toast)

Egg and Cheese Burrito

Ingredients:

-1 egg

-2 tablespoons of grated cheese

-1 whole wheat tortilla

-1/4 cup of diced tomatoes

-1 tablespoon of olive oil

Preparation Method:

-Heat the olive oil in a skillet over medium heat.

-Crack the egg into the skillet and cook for 2-3 minutes.

-Sprinkle the cheese over the egg and cook for another minute until the cheese is melted.

-Spoon the egg and cheese mixture onto the tortilla and top with the tomatoes.

-Roll up the burrito and enjoy.

Nutritional Information (per serving):

-Calories: 227

-Carbohydrates: 22g

-Protein: 11g

-Fat: 12g

Preparation Time: 10 minutes

Serving Size: 1 burrito

Ham and Cheese Breakfast Sandwich

Ingredients:

-2 slices of whole wheat bread

-2 slices of ham

-2 slices of cheese

-1 egg

-1 tablespoon of olive oil

Preparation Method:

-Heat the olive oil in a skillet over medium heat.

-Crack the egg into the skillet and cook for 2-3 minutes until set.

-Toast the bread slices and top one slice with the egg, ham, and cheese.

-Top with the second bread slice and enjoy.

Nutritional   Information   (per serving):

-Calories: 325

-Carbohydrates: 29g

-Protein: 20g

-Fat: 15g

Preparation Time: 10 minutes

Serving Size: 1 sandwich

Egg Muffins

Ingredients:

-3 eggs

-1/4 cup of diced bell pepper

-1/4 cup of diced onion

-1/4 cup of grated cheese

-1 tablespoon of olive oil

Preparation Method:

-Preheat the oven to 350°F.

-Heat the olive oil in a skillet over medium heat.

-Add the bell pepper and onion and sauté for a few minutes until softened.

-In a bowl, whisk together the eggs.

-Grease a muffin tin and divide the bell pepper and onion mixture among the cups.

-Pour the egg mixture over the vegetables and top with the cheese.

-Bake for 15-20 minutes until set in the center.

Nutritional Information (per serving):

-Calories: 122

-Carbohydrates: 2g

-Protein: 10g

-Fat: 8g

Preparation Time: 10 minutes

Serving size: 2 muffins

Mug Omelet

Ingredients:

-2 eggs

-2 tablespoons of grated cheese

-2 tablespoons of diced bell pepper

-1 tablespoon of olive oil

Preparation Method:

-Whisk together the eggs in a mug.

-Add the cheese and bell pepper.

-Heat the olive oil in a skillet over medium heat.

-Pour the egg mixture into the skillet and cook for 2-3 minutes until the edges begin to set.

-Fold the omelet in half and cook for another minute until set in the center.

Nutritional Information (per serving):

-Calories: 221

-Carbohydrates: 1g

-Protein: 13g

-Fat: 17g

Preparation Time: 10 minutes

Serving size: 2 omelets

Quinoa Porridge

Ingredients:

-1/2 cup of cooked quinoa

-1/4 cup of diced apples

-1/4 cup of diced bananas

-1/4 cup of low-fat milk

-1 teaspoon of honey

Preparation Method:

-In a saucepan, heat the quinoa and milk over medium heat.

-Stir in the apples and bananas and cook for 2-3 minutes until warmed through.

-Top with a drizzle of honey.

Nutritional Information (per serving):

-Calories: 235

-Carbohydrates: 42g

-Protein: 8g

-Fat: 4g

Preparation Time: 5 minutes

Serving Size: 1 bowl

CHAPTER 4

Snack Ideas to keep Kids with Type 1 Diabetes fueled throughout the day

Hard-boiled Eggs with a sprinkle of Sea Salt

Ingredients:
- Hard-boiled eggs
- Sea salt

Preparation Method:
- Boil eggs for 12 minutes
- Let cool and peel
- Sprinkle with sea salt

Nutritional Information (per serving):
- Calories: 79
- Fat: 6g
- Carbohydrates: 1g
- Protein: 6g

Preparation Time: 12 minutes

Serving Size: 1 hard-boiled egg

Fruit Smoothie with Greek Yogurt and Chia Seeds

Ingredients:
- 1 cup of your favorite frozen fruit
- ½ cup Greek yogurt
- ½ cup of almond milk
- 1 tablespoon of chia seeds

Preparation Method:
- Place all ingredients in a blender
- Blend for 1-2 minutes until smooth

Nutritional Information (per serving):
- Calories: 140
- Fat: 3.5g

- Carbohydrates: 20g
- Protein: 6g

Preparation Time: 5 minutes

Serving Size: 1 smoothie

Whole Wheat Toast with Almond Butter and Banana Slices

Ingredients:
- 2 slices of whole wheat bread
- 2 tablespoons of almond butter
- ½ banana, sliced

Preparation Method:
- Toast the whole wheat bread
- Spread almond butter onto the toast
- Top with banana slices

Nutritional   Information   (per serving):

- Calories: 286
- Fat: 15g
- Carbohydrates: 33g
- Protein: 8g

Preparation Time: 5 minutes

Serving Size: 2 toast slices with almond butter and banana slices

Celery Sticks with Cream Cheese and Raisins

Ingredients:
- 4 celery stalks
- 2 tablespoons of cream cheese
- 2 tablespoons of raisins

Preparation Method:
- Wash and cut the celery into sticks
- Spread cream cheese onto the celery sticks
- Top with raisins

Nutritional Information (per serving):
- Calories: 105
- Fat: 5g
- Carbohydrates: 15g
- Protein: 3g

Preparation Time: 5 minutes

Serving Size: 2 celery sticks

Hummus and Vegetables

Ingredients:
- ¼ cup of hummus
- 1 cup of your favorite vegetables (carrots, celery, cucumber, bell pepper, etc.)

Preparation Method:
- Wash and cut the vegetables into sticks
- Serve the vegetables with the hummus

Nutritional Information (per serving):
- Calories: 95
- Fat: 4.5g
- Carbohydrates: 9g
- Protein: 5g

Preparation Time: 10 minutes

Serving Size: 4 Servings

Peanut Butter and Jelly on Whole Wheat Bread

Ingredients:
- 2 slices of whole wheat bread
- 2 tablespoons of peanut butter
- 2 tablespoons of jelly

Preparation Method:

- Toast the whole wheat bread
- Spread peanut butter onto one piece of toast
- Spread jelly onto the other piece of toast
- Place the two pieces together to make a sandwich

Nutritional Information (per serving):
- Calories: 266
- Fat: 10g
- Carbohydrates: 37g
- Protein: 8g

Preparation Time: 5 minutes

Serving Size: 1 sandwich

Baked Kale Chips

Ingredients:
- 1 bunch of kale

- 2 tablespoons of olive oil
- 1 teaspoon of garlic powder
- 1 teaspoon of sea salt

Preparation Method:
- Preheat oven to 350°F
- Wash and dry the kale
- Remove the kale leaves from the stem and tear into small pieces
- Place the kale on a baking sheet and drizzle with olive oil
- Sprinkle with garlic powder and sea salt
- Bake in the oven for 10-15 minutes, until kale is crispy

Nutritional Information (per serving):
- Calories: 83
- Fat: 5g
- Carbohydrates: 6g
- Protein: 3g

Preparation Time: 25 minutes

Serving Size: 4 Servings

Popcorn with Olive Oil and a Sprinkle of Parmesan Cheese

Ingredients:
- 4 cups of popcorn
- 2 tablespoons of olive oil
- 2 tablespoons of parmesan cheese

Preparation Method:
- Place popcorn in a bowl
- Drizzle with olive oil
- Sprinkle with parmesan cheese

Nutritional Information (per serving):
- Calories: 158
- Fat: 9g
- Carbohydrates: 17g
- Protein: 4g

Preparation Time: 5 minutes

Serving size: 4 cups popcorn

Veggie Chips and Hummus

Ingredients:
- ½ cup of veggie chips
- ¼ cup of hummus

Preparation Method:
- Place the veggie chips in a bowl
- Serve with hummus

Nutritional Information (per serving):
- Calories: 135
- Fat: 7g
- Carbohydrates: 14g
- Protein: 3g

Preparation Time: 5 minutes

Serving Size: 1 bowl (½ cup of veggie chips with ¼ cup of hummus)

Whole Wheat Pretzels with Nut Butter

Ingredients:
- 1 cup of whole wheat pretzels
- 2 tablespoons of nut butter

Preparation Method:
- Place the pretzels in a bowl
- Serve with nut butter

Nutritional Information (per serving):
- Calories: 224
- Fat: 8g
- Carbohydrates: 30g
- Protein: 6g

Preparation Time: 5 minutes

Serving Size: 2 tablespoons of nut butter with 1 cup of pretzels

Baked Sweet Potato Chips with a Sprinkle of Cinnamon

Ingredients:
- 1 large sweet potato
- 2 tablespoons of olive oil
- 1 teaspoon of cinnamon

Preparation Method:
- Preheat oven to 425°F
- Wash and slice the sweet potato into thin slices
- Place the slices on a baking sheet and drizzle with olive oil
- Sprinkle with cinnamon
- Bake in the oven for 15-20 minutes, until chips are crispy

Nutritional Information (per serving):
- Calories: 120
- Fat: 7g
- Carbohydrates: 14g
- Protein: 1g

Preparation Time: 25 minutes

Serving Size: 2-3 chips

Apple Slices with Almond Butter

Ingredients:
- 1 apple, sliced
- 2 tablespoons of almond butter

Preparation Method:
- Place the apple slices in a bowl
- Serve with almond butter

Nutritional Information (per serving):
- Calories: 180
- Fat: 10g
- Carbohydrates: 20g
- Protein: 4g

Preparation Time: 5 minutes

Serving Size: 2-3 chips with 2 tablespoons of almond butter.

Turkey and Cheese Roll-Ups

Ingredients:
- 4 slices of turkey
- 4 slices of cheese

Preparation Method:
- Place a slice of cheese on top of a slice of turkey
- Roll up the turkey and cheese

Nutritional Information (per serving):
- Calories: 88
- Fat: 5g
- Carbohydrates: 0g
- Protein: 11g

Preparation Time: 5 minutes

Serving Size: 2 roll-ups

Trail Mix with Dark Chocolate Chips

Ingredients:
- ½ cup of your favorite trail mix
- 2 tablespoons of dark chocolate chips

Preparation Method:
- Place the trail mix in a bowl
- Add the dark chocolate chips

Nutritional Information (per serving):
- Calories: 166
- Fat: 9g
- Carbohydrates: 19g
- Protein: 3g

Preparation Time: 5 minutes

Serving Size: 1 cup

Cheese and Crackers

Ingredients:
- 4 crackers
- 2 tablespoons of cheese

Preparation Method:
- Place the crackers on a plate
- Top with the cheese

Nutritional Information (per serving):
- Calories: 102
- Fat: 5g
- Carbohydrates: 10g
- Protein: 4g

Preparation Time: 5 minutes

Serving Size: 1 serving (2 crackers with 2 tablespoons of cheese)

CHAPTER 5

Kid-Approved Lunch recipes for T1D

Chicken Quesadillas

Ingredients:
- 2 tablespoons vegetable oil
- 2 chicken breasts, diced
- 1 onion, diced
- 1 red bell pepper, diced
- 2 cups shredded cheese
- 8 whole wheat tortillas
- 2 tablespoons salsa

Preparation Method:
1. Heat the oil in a large skillet over medium-high heat.
2. Add the chicken, onion, and bell pepper and cook, stirring occasionally, until the chicken is cooked through and the vegetables are tender, about 8 minutes.

3. Spread 1/4 cup of the cheese over each of four of the tortillas.

4. Top each with 1/4 of the chicken mixture and then top with 1/4 cup of the remaining cheese.

5. Place the remaining four tortillas on top and press down lightly.

6. Cook in batches in the skillet over medium-high heat until the quesadillas are golden brown on both sides, about 3 minutes per side.

7. Serve with salsa.

Nutritional Information (Per Serving):

Calories: 437, Fat: 21 g, Carbohydrates: 27 g, Protein: 32 g, Fiber: 3 g, Sodium: 590 mg

Preparation Time: 20 minutes

Serving Size: 4 servings

Mediterranean Wrap

Ingredients:
- 2 tablespoons olive oil
- 2 cloves garlic, minced
- 1 red bell pepper, diced
- 1/2 cup diced tomatoes
- 1/2 teaspoon dried oregano
- 2 cups cooked chickpeas
- 2 whole wheat tortillas
- 1/2 cup crumbled feta cheese

Preparation Method:
1. Heat the oil in a large skillet over medium-high heat.

2. Add the garlic, bell pepper, tomatoes, and oregano and cook, stirring occasionally, until the vegetables are tender, about 5 minutes.

3. Add the chickpeas and cook, stirring occasionally, until heated through, about 3 minutes.

4. Spread the mixture onto the tortillas and top with feta cheese.

5. Roll up the tortillas and serve.

Nutritional Information (Per Serving):
Calories: 521, Fat: 20 g, Carbohydrates: 59 g, Protein: 23 g, Fiber: 12 g, Sodium: 604 mg

Preparation Time: 15 minutes

Serving Size: 2 wraps

Peanut Butter and Banana Sandwich

Ingredients:
- 1 tablespoon peanut butter
- 1 banana, sliced
- 2 slices whole wheat bread

Preparation Method:
1. Spread the peanut butter onto one slice of bread.
2. Top with the banana slices and the remaining slice of bread.
3. Cut in half and serve.

Nutritional Information (Per Serving):
Calories: 498, Fat: 18 g, Carbohydrates: 68 g, Protein: 15 g, Fiber: 8 g, Sodium: 412 mg

Preparation Time: 5 minutes

Serving Size: 1 sandwich

Turkey and Cheddar Sandwich

Ingredients:
- 2 tablespoons mustard
- 2 slices whole wheat bread
- 2 ounces sliced turkey

- 2 slices cheddar cheese

Preparation Method:

1. Spread the mustard onto one slice of bread.
2. Top with the turkey and cheese slices and the remaining slice of bread.
3. Cut in half and serve.

Nutritional Information (Per Serving):

Calories: 464, Fat: 18 g, Carbohydrates: 39 g, Protein: 33 g, Fiber: 4 g, Sodium: 791 mg

Preparation Time: 5 minutes

Serving Size: One sandwich

Hummus Wrap

Ingredients:
- 2 tablespoons hummus
- 1/2 cup shredded carrots

- 1/2 cup diced cucumber
- 2 whole wheat tortillas

Preparation Method:
1. Spread the hummus onto each of the tortillas.
2. Top with the carrots and cucumber.
3. Roll up the tortillas and cut in half.

Nutritional Information (Per Serving):
Calories: 542, Fat: 17 g, Carbohydrates: 71 g, Protein: 18 g, Fiber: 11 g, Sodium: 788 mg

Preparation Time: 10 minutes

Serving Size: 2 wraps

Cheese and Spinach Quesadilla

Ingredients:
- 2 tablespoons olive oil
- 1/2 onion, diced

- 2 cloves garlic, minced
- 2 cups spinach, chopped
- 2 cups shredded cheese
- 4 whole wheat tortillas

Preparation Method:
1. Heat the oil in a large skillet over medium-high heat.
2. Add the onion and garlic and cook, stirring occasionally, until softened, about 5 minutes.
3. Add the spinach and cook, stirring occasionally, until wilted, about 5 minutes.
4. Spread 1/2 cup of the cheese over each of two of the tortillas.
5. Top each with 1/2 of the spinach mixture and then top with 1/2 cup of the remaining cheese.
6. Place the remaining two tortillas on top and press down lightly.
7. Cook in batches in the skillet over medium-high heat until the quesadillas are

golden brown on both sides, about 3 minutes per side.

Nutritional Information (Per Serving):

Calories: 546, Fat: 25 g, Carbohydrates: 46 g, Protein: 28 g, Fiber: 7 g, Sodium: 681 mg

Preparation Time: 20 minutes

Serving Size: 2 Quesadillas

Egg and Cheese Sandwich

Ingredients:

- 2 tablespoons olive oil
- 2 eggs
- 2 slices whole wheat bread
- 2 slices cheddar cheese

Preparation Method:

1. Heat the oil in a large skillet over medium-high heat.
2. Crack the eggs into the skillet and cook until the whites are set and the yolks are still runny, about 2 minutes.
3. Place the eggs on one slice of bread and top with the cheese and the remaining slice of bread.
4. Cut in half and serve.

Nutritional Information (Per Serving):

Calories: 455, Fat: 24 g, Carbohydrates: 30 g, Protein: 25 g, Fiber: 3 g, Sodium: 541 mg

Preparation Time: 10 minutes

Serving size: 1 Sandwich

Veggie Wrap

Ingredients:
- 2 tablespoons olive oil
- 1 onion, diced
- 1 red bell pepper, diced
- 1/2 cup diced tomatoes
- 2 tablespoons chopped fresh parsley
- 2 whole wheat tortillas

Preparation Method:
1. Heat the oil in a large skillet over medium-high heat.
2. Add the onion and bell pepper and cook, stirring occasionally, until softened, about 5 minutes.
3. Add the tomatoes and parsley and cook, stirring occasionally, until heated through, about 3 minutes.
4. Spread the mixture onto the tortillas.
5. Roll up the tortillas and cut in half.

Nutritional Information (Per Serving):
Calories: 459, Fat: 18 g, Carbohydrates: 56 g, Protein: 13 g, Fiber: 8 g, Sodium: 598 mg

Preparation Time: 15 minutes

Serving Size: 1 wrap

Cheese Pizza

Ingredients:
- 2 tablespoons olive oil
- 1/2 onion, diced
- 1 red bell pepper, diced
- 1/2 cup pizza sauce
- 2 cups shredded cheese
- 1 pre-baked whole wheat pizza crust

Preparation Method:
1. Preheat the oven to 375°F.

2. Heat the oil in a large skillet over medium-high heat.

3. Add the onion and bell pepper and cook, stirring occasionally, until softened, about 5 minutes.

4. Spread the pizza sauce over the pizza crust.

5. Top with the onion and bell pepper mixture and then top with the cheese.

6. Bake until the cheese is melted and the crust is golden brown, about 15 minutes.

Nutritional Information (Per Serving):

Calories: 537, Fat: 24 g, Carbohydrates: 54 g, Protein: 24 g, Fiber: 6 g, Sodium: 891 mg

Preparation Time: 25 minutes

Serving size: 1 Slice

Tuna Sandwich

Ingredients:
- 2 tablespoons mayonnaise
- 1 can tuna, drained
- 2 slices whole wheat bread

Preparation Method:
1. Mix the mayonnaise and tuna together in a bowl.
2. Spread the mixture onto one slice of bread.
3. Top with the remaining slice of bread.
4. Cut in half and serve.

Nutritional Information (Per Serving):
Calories: 478, Fat: 20 g, Carbohydrates: 43 g, Protein: 28 g, Fiber: 5 g, Sodium: 711 mg

Preparation Time: 5 minutes

Serving Size: 1 sandwich (half of the prepared sandwich)

Cheesy Pasta

Ingredients:
- 2 tablespoons olive oil
- 2 cloves garlic, minced
- 1/2 onion, diced
- 1/2 teaspoon dried oregano
- 1/2 teaspoon dried basil
- 1/2 teaspoon red pepper flakes
- 1/2 cup tomato sauce
- 2 cups cooked whole wheat pasta
- 1/2 cup shredded cheese

Preparation Method:
1. Heat the oil in a large skillet over medium-high heat.
2. Add the garlic, onion, oregano, basil, and red pepper flakes and cook, stirring

occasionally, until the vegetables are softened, about 5 minutes.

3. Add the tomato sauce and pasta and cook, stirring occasionally, until heated through, about 5 minutes.

4. Stir in the cheese and cook until melted, about 2 minutes.

Nutritional Information (Per Serving):

Calories: 582, Fat: 22 g, Carbohydrates: 69 g, Protein: 28 g, Fiber: 12 g, Sodium: 594 mg

Preparation Time: 20 minutes

Serving Size: 1 cup

Egg Salad Sandwich

Ingredients:

- 2 tablespoons mayonnaise

- 3 hard-boiled eggs, chopped
- 2 slices whole wheat bread

Preparation Method:

1. Mix the mayonnaise and eggs together in a bowl.

2. Spread the mixture onto one slice of bread.

3. Top with the remaining slice of bread.

4. Cut in half and serve.

Nutritional Information (Per Serving):

Calories: 434, Fat: 23 g, Carbohydrates: 37 g, Protein: 19 g, Fiber: 5 g, Sodium: 527 mg

Preparation Time: 10 minutes

Serving Size: 1 sandwich

Macaroni and Cheese

Ingredients:
- 2 tablespoons butter
- 2 tablespoons all-purpose flour
- 1 cup milk
- 1/2 teaspoon salt
- 1/4 teaspoon pepper
- 2 cups cooked macaroni
- 1 cup shredded cheese

Preparation Method:
1. Preheat the oven to 350°F.
2. Melt the butter in a large skillet over medium-high heat.
3. Whisk in the flour and cook for 1 minute.
4. Slowly whisk in the milk and cook, stirring occasionally, until thickened, about 5 minutes.
5. Stir in the salt and pepper.
6. Add the macaroni and cheese and stir until combined.

7. Transfer to a baking dish and bake until golden brown, about 15 minutes.

Nutritional Information (Per Serving):

Calories: 517, Fat: 24 g, Carbohydrates: 51 g, Protein: 22 g, Fiber: 3 g, Sodium: 619 mg

Preparation Time: 25 minutes

Serving Size: ½ cup

Grilled Cheese Sandwich

Ingredients:
- 2 tablespoons butter
- 2 slices whole wheat bread
- 2 slices cheddar cheese

Preparation Method:

1. Heat the butter in a large skillet over medium-high heat.
2. Place the bread in the skillet and top with the cheese slices.
3. Cook until the bread is golden brown and the cheese is melted, about 3 minutes per side.
4. Cut in half and serve.

Nutritional Information (Per Serving):
Calories: 446, Fat: 24 g, Carbohydrates: 38 g, Protein: 18 g, Fiber: 4 g, Sodium: 563 mg

Preparation Time: 10 minutes

Serving Size: 1 Sandwich

Whole Wheat Pita Pizza

Ingredients:
- 2 tablespoons olive oil

- 1/2 onion, diced
- 1 red bell pepper, diced
- 1/2 cup pizza sauce
- 2 cups shredded cheese
- 2 whole wheat pita breads

Preparation Method:

1. Preheat the oven to 375°F.

2. Heat the oil in a large skillet over medium-high heat.

3. Add the onion and bell pepper and cook, stirring occasionally, until softened, about 5 minutes.

4. Spread the pizza sauce over each of the pita breads.

5. Top with the onion and bell pepper mixture and then top with the cheese.

6. Bake until the cheese is melted and the pitas are golden brown, about 15 minutes.

Nutritional Information (Per Serving):

Calories: 602, Fat: 32 g, Carbohydrates: 54 g, Protein: 28 g, Fiber: 5 g, Sodium: 850 mg

Preparation Time: 25 minutes

Serving Size: 1 Slice

CHAPTER 6

Easy Dinner Recipes for T1D kids

Macaroni and Cheese

Ingredients: 2 cups of elbow macaroni, 2 tablespoons of butter, 2 tablespoons of all-purpose flour, 1 teaspoon of dry mustard powder, 1 cup of milk, 1½ cups of shredded cheese, salt, and pepper

Preparation Method:
1. Preheat oven to 350 degrees F.
2. Cook macaroni according to package instructions.
3. Grease a 9-inch baking dish.
4. In a small saucepan, melt butter over medium heat.
5. Whisk in flour and mustard powder until combined.
6. Slowly add milk while whisking until a thick sauce forms.

7. Add cheese and stir until melted.

8. Pour sauce over macaroni and stir until combined.

9. Pour mixture into baking dish.

10. Bake for 25-30 minutes, or until golden brown and bubbly.

Nutritional Information (per serving): Calories: 318, Total fat: 16g, Saturated fat: 10g, Cholesterol: 45mg, Sodium: 491mg, Carbohydrates: 26g, Fiber: 1g, Protein: 12g,

Preparation Time: 55 minutes

Serving Size: 1 cup

Cheesy Baked Tortellini

Ingredients:
-1 package of cheese-filled tortellini
-1 jar of marinara sauce
-1 cup of shredded mozzarella cheese

-1/4 cup of grated Parmesan cheese
-Salt and pepper to taste

Preparation Method:

1. Preheat the oven to 350°F.
2. Cook the tortellini according to the package instructions.
3. Drain the tortellini and place in a baking dish.
4. Pour marinara sauce over the top of the tortellini and stir to combine.
5. Sprinkle shredded mozzarella cheese and Parmesan cheese over the top.
6. Bake for 20 minutes, or until the cheese is melted and bubbly.
7. Serve with a side salad or steamed vegetables.

Nutritional Information (per serving):

Calories: 290, Fat: 8g, Carbohydrates: 39g, Protein: 13g

Preparation Time: 25 minutes

Serving Size: About 4-6 servings

Baked Fish Fingers

Ingredients: 4 tilapia filets, 1/2 cup of plain breadcrumbs, 1/4 cup of grated Parmesan cheese, 2 tablespoons of olive oil, 1 teaspoon of garlic powder, 1 teaspoon of dried oregano, 1 teaspoon of dried basil, salt and pepper

Preparation Method:
1. Preheat oven to 400 degrees F.
2. Line a baking sheet with parchment paper.
3. In a shallow bowl, combine breadcrumbs, Parmesan cheese, garlic powder, oregano, and basil.
4. Dip each filet into the breadcrumb mixture, making sure to coat all sides.

5. Place filets on a baking sheet and drizzle with olive oil.

6. Bake for 15-20 minutes, or until golden brown and cooked through.

Nutritional Information (per serving): Calories: 246, Total fat: 10g, Saturated fat: 2g, Cholesterol: 50mg, Sodium: 260mg, Carbohydrates: 15g, Fiber: 1g, Protein: 23g

Preparation Time: 25 minutes

Serving Size: About 4-6 servings

Cheesy Broccoli Rice

Ingredients: 2 cups of cooked brown rice, 1 cup of broccoli florets, 1/4 cup of shredded cheese, 2 tablespoons of olive oil, 1 teaspoon of garlic powder, 1 teaspoon of onion powder, salt and pepper

Preparation Method:

1. Preheat oven to 350 degrees F.

2. Grease a 9-inch baking dish.

3. In a large bowl, combine cooked rice, broccoli, cheese, olive oil, garlic powder, and onion powder.

4. Pour mixture into baking dish and spread evenly.

5. Bake for 25-30 minutes, or until golden brown and cheese is melted.

Nutritional Information (per serving): Calories: 246, Total fat: 10g, Saturated fat: 2g, Cholesterol: 5mg, Sodium: 121mg, Carbohydrates: 28g, Fiber: 3g, Protein: 7g

Preparation Time: 35 minutes

Serving Size: 1 bowl

Baked Zucchini Fries

Ingredients: 2 large zucchinis, 1/2 cup of panko breadcrumbs, 1/4 cup of grated Parmesan cheese, 2 tablespoons of olive oil, 1 teaspoon of garlic powder, 1 teaspoon of dried oregano, 1 teaspoon of dried basil, salt and pepper

Preparation Method:

1. Preheat the oven to 375 degrees F.
2. Line a baking sheet with parchment paper.
3. Cut zucchinis into thin strips.
4. In a shallow bowl, combine breadcrumbs, Parmesan cheese, garlic powder, oregano, and basil.
5. Dip each zucchini strip into the breadcrumb mixture, making sure to coat all sides.
6. Place zucchini strips on a baking sheet and drizzle with olive oil.
7. Bake for 20-25 minutes, or until golden brown and crispy.

Nutritional Information (per serving): Calories: 170, Total fat: 9g, Saturated fat: 2g, Cholesterol: 4mg, Sodium: 235 mg, Carbohydrates: 10g, Fiber: 3g, Protein: 7g

Preparation Time: 30 minutes

Serving Size: 2 cups per serving

Baked Chicken Nuggets

Ingredients: 2 boneless, skinless chicken breasts, 1/2 cup of plain breadcrumbs, 2 tablespoons of olive oil, 1 teaspoon of garlic powder, 1 teaspoon of onion powder, 1 teaspoon of dried oregano, 1 teaspoon of dried basil, salt and pepper

Preparation Method:

1. Preheat the oven to 375 degrees F.

2. Line a baking sheet with parchment paper.

3. Cut chicken breasts into small strips.

4. In a shallow bowl, combine breadcrumbs, garlic powder, onion powder, oregano, and basil.

5. Dip each chicken strip into the breadcrumb mixture, making sure to coat all sides.

6. Place chicken strips on baking sheet and drizzle with olive oil.

7. Bake for 20-25 minutes, or until golden brown and cooked through.

Nutritional Information (per serving): Calories: 220, Total fat: 8g, Saturated fat: 1g, Cholesterol: 45mg, Sodium: 170mg, Carbohydrates: 17g, Fiber: 1g, Protein: 18g

Preparation Time: 25 minutes

Serving Size: 4-6 nuggets per serving

Mini Veggie Pizzas

Ingredients: 2 whole-wheat English muffins, 1/2 cup of marinara sauce, 1/4 cup of shredded cheese, 1/4 cup of diced bell peppers, 1/4 cup of diced mushrooms, 1/4 cup of diced onions, 2 tablespoons of olive oil, 1 teaspoon of garlic powder, salt and pepper

Preparation Method:
1. Preheat oven to 375 degrees F.
2. Line a baking sheet with parchment paper.
3. Split English muffins in half and place on baking sheet.
4. Top with marinara sauce, cheese, bell peppers, mushrooms, and onions.

5. Drizzle with olive oil and sprinkle with garlic powder.

6. Bake for 15-20 minutes, or until English muffins are golden brown and cheese is melted.

Nutritional Information (per serving): Calories: 237, Total fat: 10g, Saturated fat: 2g, Cholesterol: 5mg, Sodium: 350mg, Carbohydrates: 25g, Fiber: 4g, Protein: 9g

Preparation Time: 25 minutes

Serving Size: one mini pizza per meal.

Turkey Sloppy Joes

Ingredients: 1 pound of ground turkey, 1/4 cup of diced onions, 1/4 cup of diced bell peppers, 1/4 cup of diced mushrooms, 1/2 cup of ketchup, 2 tablespoons of

Worcestershire sauce, 1 teaspoon of garlic powder, 1 teaspoon of onion powder, 1 teaspoon of cumin, salt and pepper

Preparation Method:
1. Preheat a large skillet over medium heat.
2. Add ground turkey and cook for 5-7 minutes, or until cooked through.
3. Add onions, bell peppers, and mushrooms and cook for an additional 3-4 minutes, or until vegetables are tender.
4. Add ketchup, Worcestershire sauce, garlic powder, onion powder, and cumin and stir until combined.
5. Simmer for 10 minutes, or until sauce has thickened.

Nutritional Information (per serving): Calories: 309, Total fat: 13g, Saturated fat: 4g, Cholesterol: 79mg, Sodium: 917 mg, Carbohydrates: 19g, Fiber: 2g, Protein: 29g

Preparation Time: 25 minutes

Serving Size: ½ cup

Baked Chicken Tenders

Ingredients: 2 boneless, skinless chicken breasts, 1/2 cup of plain breadcrumbs, 2 tablespoons of olive oil, 1 teaspoon of garlic powder, 1 teaspoon of onion powder, 1 teaspoon of dried oregano, 1 teaspoon of dried basil, salt and pepper

Preparation Method:
1. Preheat the oven to 375 degrees F.
2. Line a baking sheet with parchment paper.
3. Cut chicken breasts into thin strips.
4. In a shallow bowl, combine breadcrumbs, garlic powder, onion powder, oregano, and basil.

5. Dip each chicken strip into the breadcrumb mixture, making sure to coat all sides.

6. Place chicken strips on baking sheet and drizzle with olive oil.

7. Bake for 20-25 minutes, or until golden brown and cooked through.

Nutritional Information (per serving): Calories: 220, Total fat: 8g, Saturated fat: 1g, Cholesterol: 45mg, Sodium: 170mg, Carbohydrates: 17g, Fiber: 1g, Protein: 18g

Preparation Time: 25 minutes

Serving Size: 2-3 chicken tenders

Grilled Cheese Sandwiches

Ingredients: 4 slices of whole-wheat bread, 4 slices of cheese, 2 tablespoons of butter

Preparation Method:

1. Preheat a large skillet over medium heat.

2. Spread one side of each slice of bread with butter.

3. Place two slices of bread in the skillet, butter side down.

4. Top with one slice of cheese and the remaining slices of bread, butter side up.

5. Cook for 3-4 minutes, or until golden brown.

6. Flip sandwiches and cook for an additional 3-4 minutes, until the cheese is melted.

Nutritional Information (per serving): Calories: 262, Total fat: 14g, Saturated fat: 8g, Cholesterol: 30mg, Sodium: 443 mg, Carbohydrates: 23g, Fiber: 3g, Protein: 11g

Preparation Time: 10 minutes
Serving Size: 2 sandwiches per meal

Roasted Vegetables

Ingredients: 2 cups of diced potatoes, 1 cup of diced bell peppers, 1 cup of diced carrots, 1 cup of diced onions, 2 tablespoons of olive oil, 1 teaspoon of garlic powder, 1 teaspoon of dried oregano, 1 teaspoon of dried basil, salt and pepper

Preparation Method:
1. Preheat the oven to 375 degrees F.
2. Line a baking sheet with parchment paper.
3. Spread vegetables on a baking sheet and drizzle with olive oil.
4. Sprinkle it with garlic powder, oregano, and basil.
5. Bake for 25-30 minutes, or until vegetables are tender and golden brown.

Nutritional Information (per serving): Calories: 145, Total fat: 4g,

Saturated fat: 1g, Cholesterol: 0mg, Sodium: 74mg, Carbohydrates: 24g, Fiber: 5g, Protein: 3g

Preparation Time: 30 minutes

Serving Size: 1 bowl

Baked Potato Wedges

Ingredients: 4 large potatoes, 2 tablespoons of olive oil, 1 teaspoon of garlic powder, 1 teaspoon of onion powder, 1 teaspoon of dried oregano, 1 teaspoon of dried basil, salt and pepper

Preparation Method:
1. Preheat oven to 375 degrees F.
2. Line a baking sheet with parchment paper.
3. Cut potatoes into wedges.

4. Spread wedges on baking sheet and drizzle with olive oil.

5. Sprinkle with garlic powder, onion powder, oregano, and basil.

6. Bake for 25-30 minutes, or until golden brown and crispy.

Nutritional Information (per serving): Calories: 205, Total fat: 6g, Saturated fat: 1g, Cholesterol: 0mg, Sodium: 47mg, Carbohydrates: 10g, Fiber: 5g, Protein: 4g

Preparation Time: 30 minutes

Serving Size: 1-2 wedges per meal

Baked Sweet Potato Fries

Ingredients: 2 large sweet potatoes, 2 tablespoons of olive oil, 1 teaspoon of garlic powder, 1 teaspoon of onion powder, 1

teaspoon of dried oregano, 1 teaspoon of dried basil, salt and pepper

Preparation Method:

1. Preheat oven to 375 degrees F.
2. Line a baking sheet with parchment paper.
3. Cut sweet potatoes into thin strips.
4. Spread sweet potato strips on baking sheet and drizzle with olive oil.
5. Sprinkle with garlic powder, onion powder, oregano, and basil.
6. Bake for 25-30 minutes, or until golden brown and crispy.

Nutritional Information (per serving): Calories: 186, Total fat: 7g, Saturated fat: 1g, Cholesterol: 0mg, Sodium: 38mg, Carbohydrates: 27g, Fiber: 5g, Protein: 3g

Preparation Time: 30 minutes
Serving Size: 1 Cup

Creamy Chicken Alfredo

Ingredients: 2 cups of cooked fettuccine, 2 boneless, skinless chicken breasts, 2 tablespoons of butter, 2 tablespoons of all-purpose flour, 1 cup of milk, 1/2 cup of grated Parmesan cheese, 1 teaspoon of garlic powder, 1 teaspoon of dried oregano, 1 teaspoon of dried basil, salt and pepper

Preparation Method:
1. Preheat a large skillet over medium heat.
2. Add chicken breasts and cook for 5-7 minutes, or until cooked through.
3. Remove chicken from skillet and set aside.
4. Melt butter in the skillet and whisk in flour until combined.
5. Slowly add milk while whisking until a thick sauce forms.

6. Add Parmesan cheese, garlic powder, oregano, and basil and stir until cheese is melted.

7. Add cooked chicken and cooked fettuccine and stir until combined.

Nutritional Information (per serving): Calories: 507, Total fat: 19g, Saturated fat: 10g, Cholesterol: 79mg, Sodium: 463 mg, Carbohydrates: 48g, Fiber: 3g, Protein: 35g

Preparation Time: 25 minutes

Serving size: 1 cup sauce

CHAPTER 7

Satisfying Type 1 Diabetes-friendly Desserts for kids

Banana Split

Ingredients:
-2 ripe bananas
-1/2 cup plain low-fat yogurt
-1/4 cup diced strawberries
-1/4 cup blueberries
-2 tablespoons chopped walnuts
-1 teaspoon pure vanilla extract

Preparation Method:
1. Cut the bananas in half lengthwise and place them in a shallow bowl.
2. Top with yogurt, strawberries, blueberries and walnuts.
3. Drizzle with vanilla extract and serve.

Nutritional Information (per serving):

Calories: 150
Carbohydrates: 20 g
Total fat: 5 g
Saturated fat: 0.5 g
Cholesterol: 0 mg
Sodium: 15 mg
Fiber: 4 g
Protein: 5 g

Preparation Time: 5 minutes

Serving Instructions:

• Serve the banana split with whole-wheat bread or crackers on the side.

• To aid reduce the absorption of sugar, provide a glass of milk or water.

• Before, during, and after eating the banana split, have your kid check their blood sugar.

Baked Apple

Ingredients:
-1 large apple
-1 tablespoon brown sugar
-1 teaspoon cinnamon
-1 teaspoon butter
-1 tablespoon raisins

Preparation Method:
1. Preheat oven to 350 degrees F.
2. Core apple and place in a baking dish.
3. In a small bowl, mix together brown sugar, cinnamon and butter.
4. Spread mixture over the top of the apple and sprinkle with raisins.
5. Bake in a preheated oven for 30 minutes, or until the apple is tender.

Nutritional Information (per serving):
Calories: 140
Carbohydrates: 5 g
Total fat: 3 g

Saturated fat: 1.5 g
Cholesterol: 5 mg
Sodium: 10 mg
Fiber: 5 g
Protein: 1 g

Preparation Time: 5 minutes

Serving Size: 1 baked apple per serving

Chocolate Peanut Butter Rice Krispie Treats

Ingredients:
-3 tablespoons butter
-1/4 cup peanut butter
-2 cups mini marshmallows
-3 cups Rice Krispies cereal
-1/4 cup semi-sweet chocolate chips

Preparation Method:

1. In a large saucepan, melt butter and peanut butter over medium-low heat.

2. Add marshmallows and stir until melted.

3. Remove from heat and stir in Rice Krispies cereal.

4. Spread mixture into a greased 9x13 inch baking dish.

5. Sprinkle chocolate chips and press into the cereal mixture.

6. Allow to cool before cutting into bars.

Nutritional Information (per serving):

Calories: 140
Carbohydrates: 14 g
Total fat: 6 g
Saturated fat: 3 g
Cholesterol: 5 mg
Sodium: 70 mg
Fiber: 1 g
Protein: 2 g

Preparation Time: 10 minutes

Serving Size: 1 bowl

Apple Pie Crisp

Ingredients:
-4 cups diced apples
-1/4 cup brown sugar
-1/4 cup white sugar
-1/4 cup rolled oats
-1/4 cup whole wheat flour
-1/4 teaspoon ground cinnamon
-1/4 teaspoon ground nutmeg
-2 tablespoons melted butter

Preparation Method:
1. Preheat oven to 350 degrees F.
2. Place apples in a greased 9x13 inch baking dish.
3. In a small bowl, mix together brown sugar, white sugar, oats, flour, cinnamon and nutmeg.
4. Sprinkle over the top of the apples.

5. Drizzle with melted butter.

6. Bake in a preheated oven for 30-35 minutes, or until golden brown.

Nutritional Information (per serving):

Calories: 140
Carbohydrates: 30 g
Total fat: 5 g
Saturated fat: 3 g
Cholesterol: 10 mg
Sodium: 10 mg
Fiber: 2 g
Protein: 2 g

Preparation Time: 35 minutes
Serving Size: ½ cup

Chocolate Peanut Butter Banana Popsicles

Ingredients:

-3 ripe bananas

-1/4 cup smooth peanut butter
-1/4 cup semi-sweet chocolate chips
-1/4 cup chopped peanuts

Preparation Method:
1. Peel bananas and cut into 1-inch slices.
2. Place slices on a parchment-lined baking sheet and freeze for 1 hour.
3. In a small bowl, melt peanut butter and chocolate chips in the microwave.
4. Dip banana slices into the melted mixture and sprinkle with chopped peanuts.
5. Place back onto the baking sheet and freeze for another hour.
6. Serve.

Nutritional Information (per serving):
Calories: 150
Carbohydrates: 10 g
Total fat: 10 g
Saturated fat: 3 g
Cholesterol: 0 mg

Sodium: 10 mg
Fiber: 2 g
Protein: 5 g

Preparation Time: 2 hours

Serving Size: 1 popsicle

Oatmeal Raisin Cookies

Ingredients:
-1 cup quick-cooking oats
-1/2 cup whole wheat flour
-1/2 teaspoon baking soda
-1/4 teaspoon salt
-1/4 cup melted butter
-1/4 cup brown sugar
-1/4 cup honey
-1 teaspoon vanilla extract
-1/4 cup raisins

Preparation Method:

1. Preheat oven to 350 degrees F.

2. In a medium bowl, mix together oats, flour, baking soda and salt.

3. In a separate bowl, cream together butter, brown sugar, honey and vanilla extract until light and fluffy.

4. Slowly add dry ingredients to the wet ingredients and mix until well combined.

5. Stir in raisins.

6. Drop spoonfuls of cookie dough onto a greased baking sheet.

7. Bake in preheated oven for 12-15 minutes, or until golden brown.

Nutritional Information (per serving):

Calories: 140

Carbohydrates: 30 g

Total fat: 5 g

Saturated fat: 2.5 g

Cholesterol: 10 mg

Sodium: 95 mg

Fiber: 2 g

Protein: 2 g

Preparation Time: 15 minutes
Serving Size: 3 - 4 cookies

Coconut Macaroons

Ingredients:
-2 egg whites
-1/4 cup honey
-1/4 teaspoon almond extract
-1/4 teaspoon salt
-1/4 cup unsweetened coconut flakes
-1/4 cup chopped almonds

Preparation Method:
1. Preheat oven to 350 degrees F.
2. In a medium bowl, beat together egg whites, honey, almond extract and salt until frothy.
3. Fold in coconut flakes and chopped almonds.

4. Drop spoonfuls of the mixture onto a greased baking sheet.

5. Bake in preheated oven for 15 minutes, or until golden brown.

Nutritional Information (per serving):

Calories: 70

Carbohydrates: 15 g

Total fat: 5 g

Saturated fat: 2 g

Cholesterol: 0 mg

Sodium: 25 mg

Fiber: 1 g

Protein: 2 g

Preparation Time: 15 minutes

Serving Size: 1-2 macaroons per serving

Fruit Pizza

Ingredients:

-1/2 cup plain Greek yogurt
-1 teaspoon honey
-1/4 cup diced strawberries
-1/4 cup diced kiwi
-1/4 cup diced pineapple
-1/4 cup blueberries
-1/4 cup chopped almonds

Preparation Method:

1. Preheat oven to 350 degrees F.
2. In a bowl, mix together yogurt and honey.
3. Spread mixture onto a greased 9-inch pizza pan.
4. Top with strawberries, kiwi, pineapple and blueberries.
5. Sprinkle with chopped almonds.
6. Bake in preheated oven for 15 minutes, or until golden brown.

Nutritional Information (per serving):

Calories: 140
Carbohydrates: 20 g
Total fat: 5 g
Saturated fat: 1 g
Cholesterol: 5 mg
Sodium: 65 mg
Fiber: 3 g
Protein: 6 g

Preparation Time: 15 minutes

Serving Size: 2 slices per serving

Chocolate Banana Boats

Ingredients:
-2 ripe bananas
-1/4 cup semi-sweet chocolate chips
-2 tablespoons chopped walnuts

Preparation Method:

1. Slice bananas in half lengthwise and place on a parchment-lined baking sheet.

2. Sprinkle it with chocolate chips and walnuts.

3. Bake in a preheated oven at 350 degrees F for 10 minutes.

4. Serve.

Nutritional Information (per serving):

Calories: 130

Carbohydrates: 12 g

Total fat: 5 g

Saturated fat: 2 g

Cholesterol: 0 mg

Sodium: 0 mg

Fiber: 3 g

Protein: 2 g

Preparation Time: 10 minutes

Serving Size: ½ cup

Fruit and Yogurt Parfait

Ingredients:
-1/2 cup plain Greek yogurt
-1/4 cup diced strawberries
-1/4 cup diced kiwi
-1/4 cup diced pineapple
-1/4 cup blueberries
-1/4 cup chopped almonds

Preparation Method:
1. Place yogurt in a bowl.
2. Top with strawberries, kiwi, pineapple, blueberries and almonds.
3. Serve.

Nutritional Information (per serving):
Calories: 140
Total fat: 6 g
Saturated fat: 1 g
Cholesterol: 5 mg

Sodium: 20 mg
Fiber: 2 g
Protein: 5 g

Preparation Time: 5 minutes

Serving Size: 1 parfait

Chocolate-Dipped Strawberries

Ingredients:
-1/2 cup semi-sweet chocolate chips
-1/4 cup coconut oil
-1/4 teaspoon vanilla extract
-1/4 teaspoon almond extract
-1 pint strawberries

Preparation Method:
1. In a small bowl, melt chocolate chips and coconut oil in the microwave.
2. Stir in vanilla and almond extracts.

3. Dip strawberries into the melted chocolate mixture.
4. Place on a parchment-lined baking sheet and refrigerate for 30 minutes.
5. Serve.

Nutritional Information (per serving):
Calories: 140
Total fat: 8 g
Saturated fat: 5 g
Cholesterol: 0 mg
Sodium: 0 mg
Fiber: 2 g
Protein: 1 g

Preparation Time: 35 minutes

Serving Size: 2-3 strawberries per serving.

Chocolate Peanut Butter Fudge

Ingredients:
-1/2 cup creamy peanut butter
-1/4 cup butter
-1/4 cup honey
-1/4 cup cocoa powder
-1 teaspoon vanilla extract

Preparation Method:
1. Grease a 9x9 inch baking dish.
2. In a medium saucepan, melt peanut butter, butter and honey over medium heat.
3. Remove from heat and stir in cocoa powder and vanilla extract.
4. Pour into prepared baking dish and refrigerate for 1 hour.
5. Cut into squares and serve.

Nutritional Information (per serving):
Calories: 170

Carbohydrates: 14 g
Total fat: 5 g
Saturated fat: 5 g
Cholesterol: 0 mg
Sodium: 20 mg
Fiber: 1 g
Protein: 4 g

Preparation Time: 1 hour 10 minutes
Serving Size: 1 square

Cinnamon Apple Chips

Ingredients:
-2 large apples
-1 teaspoon cinnamon
-1 teaspoon sugar

Preparation Method:
1. Preheat oven to 350 degrees F.
2. Slice apples into thin slices and place on a parchment-lined baking sheet.

3. Sprinkle with cinnamon and sugar.

4. Bake in preheated oven for 20 minutes, or until crisp.

Nutritional Information (per serving):

Calories: 90

Total fat: 0 g

Saturated fat: 0 g

Cholesterol: 0 mg

Sodium: 0 mg

Fiber: 4 g

Protein: 0 g

Preparation Time: 20 minutes

Serving Size: 10 - 15 chips

Peanut Butter and Jelly Bars

Ingredients:
-3/4 cup whole wheat flour
-1/2 teaspoon baking soda
-1/2 teaspoon baking powder
-1/4 teaspoon salt
-3/4 cup peanut butter
-1/4 cup melted butter
-1/4 cup honey
-1 teaspoon vanilla extract
-1/4 cup jelly

Preparation Method:
1. Preheat oven to 350 degrees F.
2. In a medium bowl, mix together flour, baking soda, baking powder and salt.
3. In a separate bowl, cream together peanut butter, butter, honey and vanilla extract until light and fluffy.
4. Slowly add dry ingredients to the wet ingredients and mix until well combined.
5. Spread mixture into a greased 9x13 inch baking dish.

6. Spread jelly over the top.

7. Bake in preheated oven for 20 minutes, or until golden brown.

Nutritional Information (per serving):

Calories: 140

Total fat: 9 g

Saturated fat: 3 g

Cholesterol: 10 mg

Sodium: 90 mg

Fiber: 1 g

Protein: 3 g

Preparation Time: 20 minutes

Serving Size: 2 bars

CHAPTER 8

Dealing with Eating outside the home with your T1D kids

Eating outside the home with your Type 1 Diabetes Kids can be a daunting task. Parents of kids with Type 1 Diabetes (T1D) have to be especially mindful of not only what they are eating but also how they're managing the diabetes while away from home. Eating away from home can present challenges for kids with T1D, so it's important for parents to be prepared and know what to expect.

One of the most important things to consider when eating away from home with your Type 1 Diabetes Kids is meal planning. IIaving a plan for what your child will eat can help to make sure their blood sugar levels stay in a healthy range. It's important to make sure that the meals are balanced, meaning that they contain a combination of carbohydrates, proteins, and fats. Additionally, it's important to choose foods that are lower in added sugar and that won't cause rapid spikes in blood sugar.

Once you've identified meals that are appropriate, it's important to plan ahead and pack food if necessary. This can help to ensure that your child has access to healthy food options while away from home. When packing food, it's important to keep it cool and safe. If possible, it's best to pack food that doesn't need to be refrigerated or heated up. This will help to reduce the risk of food-borne illness.

When eating out, it's important to be mindful of the portion sizes. Eating too much can lead to high blood sugar levels, so it's important to portion out the food accordingly. Additionally, it's important to be mindful of any hidden sugars. Many restaurants use added sugars in their sauces and dressings, so be sure to ask about the ingredients before ordering.

It's also important to be mindful of the timing of meals. Eating outside the home can be unpredictable and can cause delays in meals. This can be especially problematic for kids with Type 1 Diabetes. If possible, it's important to plan meals so that they are spaced out throughout the day. Additionally, it's important to make sure that snacks are available in case there are delays in meals.

When dealing with Type 1 Diabetes, it's also important to be prepared for any unexpected blood sugar levels. Having a plan for how to handle low or high blood sugar levels can help to ensure that your child is safe. It's also important to make sure that your child has access to their diabetes supplies, such as insulin, glucose tablets, and test strips.

Being prepared for eating outside the home with your Type 1 Diabetes Kids can help to reduce stress and ensure that your child's diabetes is managed safely. With proper planning and preparation, it's possible to have a successful and enjoyable experience while eating away from home.

Finally, it's important to remember that eating outside the home doesn't have to be stressful. With proper planning and preparation, you can ensure that your child has access to healthy meal options and can safely manage their diabetes while away from home.

CHAPTER 9

Coping mechanisms for parents of kids with T1D

Caring for a child with type 1 diabetes (T1D) can be an overwhelming and stressful experience for parents. It requires a great deal of time and effort to manage the condition, and parents often struggle to find ways to cope. While there is no one-size-fits-all solution, there are many strategies that parents can use to help them cope with the demands of caring for a child with T1D.

In this chapter, we'll discuss some of the common coping mechanisms for parents of children with T1D. We'll look at strategies that can help parents manage the stress and emotions associated with caring for a child with T1D. We'll also provide some tips for helping parents build a strong support system.

1. Acknowledge Your Emotions

It's normal for parents of children with T1D to have a range of emotions, from guilt and frustration to anxiety and fear. It's important to acknowledge and validate these feelings instead of trying to push them away. Talking to a trusted friend or family member can be a great way to express your emotions and get support. It's also important to take time for yourself to relax and unwind.

2. Create A Support System

Having a strong support system is essential for parents of children with T1D. It's important to build a network of people who can provide emotional, practical, and financial support. This could include close friends, family members, and other parents of children with T1D. Professionals such as doctors, nurses, and mental health providers can also be part of your support system.

3. Practice Self-Care

It's important for parents to take time for themselves and practice self-care. This can include activities such as exercising, meditating, or engaging in a hobby. Taking care of your own physical, mental, and emotional health can help you better care for your child.

4. Learn About T1D

It's important to educate yourself about T1D so that you can better understand your child's condition and how to manage it. Talk to your child's healthcare providers and read up on the latest research. You can also join support groups and connect with other parents of children with T1D.

5. Set Realistic Goals

Setting realistic goals can help you stay on track and manage your stress levels. Focus on setting achievable goals and breaking big tasks into manageable chunks. It's also important to be realistic about what you can handle on any given day and to recognize when you need a break.

6. Talk to Your Child

Talking to your child about T1D can help you both better understand the condition and how to manage it. Make sure to explain the condition in terms that your child can understand and create a plan for managing it. It's also important to be honest with your child about the challenges of living with T1D.

7. Seek Professional Help

If you're feeling overwhelmed or struggling to cope, you should consider seeking professional help. Talking to a therapist or counselor can help you better manage your emotions and cope with the demands of caring for a child with T1D.

Caring for a child with T1D can be an overwhelming and stressful experience. While there is no one-size-fits-all solution, there are many strategies that parents can use to help them cope. From acknowledging your emotions to seeking professional help, these coping strategies can help parents manage the demands of caring for a child with T1D.

CHAPTER 10

Conclusion and Additional Resources for Families of Kids with Type 1 Diabetes

Families of kids with type 1 diabetes have a lot to consider when it comes to managing their child's condition. It is important to understand the necessary basics of diabetes management, such as checking blood sugar levels, adjusting insulin doses, and eating healthy meals. It is also important to understand the emotional impact of type 1 diabetes and how it can affect a child's overall well-being.

It is essential for parents to be proactive in helping their child manage their diabetes in order to ensure long-term health. This includes finding the right healthcare team, setting up a daily routine, and being aware of the warning signs of diabetes-related complications. Parents should also be aware of the available resources and support systems that can help them navigate this difficult but manageable condition.

Additional Resources

1. American Diabetes Association: This non-profit organization provides helpful information about type 1 diabetes and offers a range of resources for families of kids with diabetes. This includes information about diabetes management, nutrition, research, and advocacy.

2. Centers for Disease Control and Prevention: This government website provides evidence-based information about type 1 diabetes and offers helpful tips for managing the condition.

3. National Institutes of Health: This website provides evidence-based information and resources about type 1 diabetes, including information about research, clinical trials, and treatments.

4. JDRF (Juvenile Diabetes Research Foundation): This non-profit organization focuses on type 1 diabetes research and provides resources for families of kids with type 1 diabetes.

5. Children with Diabetes: This website provides a range of resources to help families of kids with type 1 diabetes, including information about diabetes management, nutrition, and emotional support.

6. American Academy of Pediatrics: This website provides evidence-based information about diabetes management

and offers resources for parents of kids with
type 1 diabetes

To learn more about diabetes, get my
other books on the subject.

Diabetes Education

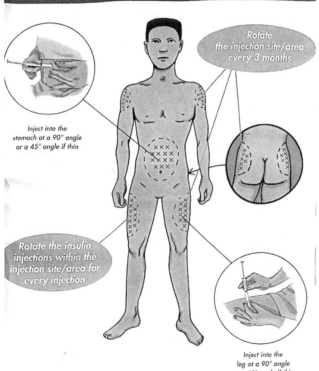

DIABETES EDUCATION
Injection Sites and Technique

Rotate
the injection site/area
every 3 months

Inject into the
stomach at a 90° angle
or a 45° angle if thin

Rotate the insulin
injections within the
injection site/area for
every injection

Inject into the
leg at a 90° angle
or a 45° angle if thin

Diabetes Foot Care Education

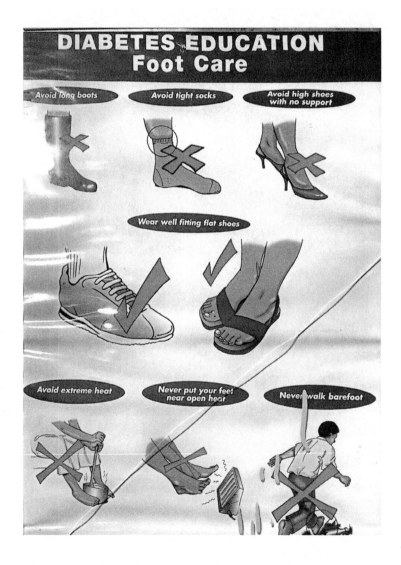

BONUS

14 Days Meal Planner

DAYS	RECIPES	REMARKS
1		
2		
3		

4		
5		
6		
7		
8		

9		
10		
11		
12		

13		
14		
15		

Thank You Note

Dear Reader,

Thank you so much for buying and reading my Type 1 diabetes cookbook for kids!
Hope you and your child have found the recipes to be both delicious and nutritious. I know that managing Type 1 diabetes can be challenging, but I hope that this cookbook has made it a lot easier.

A lot of time and effort has been put into creating this cookbook, and I'm so glad that you found it helpful. ***If you had a positive experience with the cookbook, I would be grateful if you would consider leaving a 5-star rating ⭐ on Amazon.*** Your feedback will go a long way in helping other families find this resource, and it means a lot to me.

Thank you again for your support!

Sincerely,

Sonia Russell

Printed in Great Britain
by Amazon

38403669R00096